THE PROPERTY INSURANCE B.I.B.L.E

A GUIDE TO GETTING *B*ETTER HOME *I*NSURANCE *B*EFORE *L*OSING *E*VERYTHING

ABRAHAM KEVIN SPANN

Copyright © 2022 Abraham Kevin Spann

ISBN 979-8-9857877-4-0 (paperback)

JM Publishing

All rights reserved. No part of this book may be reproduced, stored, or transmitted by any means—whether auditory, graphic, mechanical, or electronic—without written permission of both publisher and author, except in the case of brief excerpts used in critical articles and reviews. Unauthorized reproduction of any part of this work is illegal and is punishable by law.

Printed in the United States of America

DEDICATION

To the loving memory of my parents, Robert and Rosa Spann.

OUTLINE

Dedication iii

Foreword vii

Acknowledgments xi

Introduction xiii

    1.   The Dream of Homeownership 1

    2.   The Choice is Yours 9

    3.   The Value of a Great Relationship 19

    4.   Home is Where the Heart is 27

    5.   Let's Talk About Claims 41

    6.   Natural Disasters 53

    7.   The Annual Policy Review 65

Epilogue 77

FOREWORD

My father said, "When my son is born, call him Abraham." My mother named me Kevin. He always called me "Abby," and it's a level of exclusivity that I'll never share with anyone else. I'm the sixth of seven children, from the union of my parents, Robert and Rosa Spann. My older siblings taught me to read and do math before I started school. As far back as I can remember, my extended family of aunts, uncles, and first cousins encouraged me to entertain them with my math acumen. I guess you can say I was raised to be a mathlete, not an athlete. Someone would say, "Ask Little Kevin to do addition." A relative would begin posing math problems to me. "What's one plus one?" "Two," I answered. "Two plus two?" he asked. "Four," I responded. This would continue into the thousands or until the person asking was bored or no longer sure if I was giving the right answers.

I attended the Wyandanch Head Start program where my mother worked. When it was time to go to kindergarten, my mother fought the school administration and insisted they put me in first grade. Her persistence paid off. I skipped kindergarten and was always the youngest in my class. Her love and support are a quiet confidence that I carry with me into every room that I enter. My mother smiled proudly when I won the math contests in Milton L. Olive Middle School. When I went away to college, I called my mother every Sunday night—religiously, without fail. Once a year, an incident would happen that would make me feel like dropping out. She always reminded me who I was and not to let anyone make me stray from my destiny. When I graduated from Rochester Institute of Technology—she was right there—we did it. Thanks Ma.

Joseph Spann, my paternal grandfather, was a sharecropper. My father was raised in Pinewood, South Carolina with a farmer's work ethic. He started Robert A. Spann & Sons Floor Waxing and Office Cleaning company the year I was born. At the age of eight, I followed the lead of my older siblings and began working in the family business. My brother, Robert A. Spann Jr. runs the business to this day, almost sixty years later. My insurance agency is named "Abraham Kevin Spann & Sons, Inc.," as a tribute to my father. Daddy was a reader, a quiet leader, and a man of great integrity. Always an early riser, we had some jobs that we did at 5:30 in the morning before school started and other jobs that we handled late in the evening after the clients had gone home from the office. "Work when you have a mind to work," is one of many lessons that stayed with me to this day. Daddy, you'd be proud to know that most of this book was written at 5:00 in the morning, before I started work.

This book is dedicated to the loving memory of Robert A. Spann and Rosa Spann. I was blessed to have my dad in my life for forty years until his passing in 2003. I'm eternally grateful to God for letting me have my mom for fifty years until her passing, three days after my fiftieth birthday. I included the B.I.B.L.E. acronym in the title to honor my parents as people of great faith.

ACKNOWLEDGMENTS

Special thanks and appreciation to my siblings, Lenore Walters, Beatrice Hamilton, Robertha Johnson, Robert Spann, Jr., Theresa Johnson, and Nadine Spann. To my maternal Walters side of my family and my paternal Spann side of my family—you know the roles you played in my life, and I'm forever grateful. To the Certains, especially the matriarch, Grace Certain—I think we crossed the bridge many years ago where we are no longer "in-laws." We are just family. I have too many nieces and nephews to list by name, but you know that Uncle Kevin loves and appreciates you greatly.

Lastly, my wife, Denise. We laughed and cried together already when we saw the first version of the book cover. You know our journey. You know how we started. You took a leap of faith with me, Allstate, and the insurance industry—when you said "Yes, I'll leave all that I know and love and move to Chicago with you." You also knew when it was time to start packing and come back home, long before we had anything steady lined up. I'm forever grateful and eternally indebted to you for our sons, Abraham Kevin II, Dominique Kiwane, and Trey Robert Matthew. Kevy,

ACKNOWLEDGMENTS

Nico, and Trey, all of you are better versions of me—no, let me restate that—you guys are our ancestors' wildest dreams. Finally, my grandchildren, Jade Madison Spann and Mason Levi Spann, guess what? Pop-Pop wrote a book!

INTRODUCTION

People who have recently met me through social media only know me as "Kevin Spann, the Insurance Guru." It is a great tagline for digital branding, reels, YouTube, and my frequent appearances as a guest or host on podcasts, but my journey in the insurance industry didn't start that way.

I entered the insurance industry at age twenty-four and never looked back. At the time, I was newly married and the proud father of my first son. Thirty-five years later, I'm still happily married to my beautiful wife, Denise. Our family has grown to include three sons, Kevin II, Dominique, Trey, and two grandchildren, Jade (granddaughter) and Mason (grandson).

The first twenty years of my career were spent building my expertise as a company employee. I started as a Life Underwriter Trainee in Melville, New York. Four years later the company moved my family and I to Chicago to manage a team. Hard work and dedication took me from managing a staff of ten people to a full division with over sixty employees.

Introduction

Ten years into my career, I pivoted from Operations to an Agency Sales Manager Trainee. Early mornings and late nights, led to immediate success as a Sales Manager and Market Business Consultant. I thoroughly enjoyed recruiting new agents as well as helping existing agents develop strategies and techniques to improve their performance. I was highly successful at making others highly successful, but why didn't I have my own agency?

In 2007, I walked away from all the comforts of corporate America—great salary, benefits, company car, and a GAS CARD and I began a new relationship with my same company as an Exclusive Agent/Independent Contractor. I took a leap of faith and bet on myself. I purchased my first agency in 2007, my second in 2009, my third in 2011, and recently closed on the purchase of my fourth agency in June 2022.

"I love what I do" is an understatement to how I feel about my profession. As a multi-line insurance agent, I get to help people insure their dreams. Not cars, not houses, not businesses—dreams. Today, I lead a staff of licensed insurance agents and partner with other professionals in the Dream Business: Realtors, Lenders, CPAs, Attorneys, and a host of others. My passion for the backstory (How did you buy this apartment? House? Investment Property?) is unmatched. My passion for making sure people and their dreams are properly insured is even greater!

"Insure Your Dreams - The Kevin Spann Brand" is the answer to the question that you never asked. "How can I make sure that everything I have worked so hard to get is properly insured so I can't lose it to an accident, a catastrophe, lawsuit, or natural disaster?"

I, Abraham "Kevin" Spann, am a thirty-five-year veteran of the insurance industry. My award-winning agency has been recognized nationally for top performance as well as my drive and dedication to giving back to the community.

I vividly remember the days of walking the streets of Wyandanch (Long Island), New York, looking at all the houses and thinking, *Everybody that owns these homes can't all be better than me. I have to be able to earn a good enough living to buy a house for my family and myself.* Marrying at age twenty-two and becoming a father a week later, the economic realities of my dream were deferred, but not denied.

In 1987, I was hired to work at Allstate Insurance Company as a Life Underwriter Trainee. Four months later, my young family and I were able to leave the comfort of my mother-in-law's home to rent our first apartment. Hard work led to several promotions and ultimately a relocation to Chicago, Illinois in 1991. Sitting in a barbershop, I saw an ad:

New Construction

$89,000 - $129,000
Only 3% down

Introduction

A natural "mathlete" since birth, I quickly calculated that I only needed about $3,000 down, and I could buy a home! The momentary euphoria simmered down when I remembered that I had less than a hundred dollars in the bank. Now what?

I shared the excitement with my wife, Denise, who was five months pregnant with our second child. Always optimistic, we met with the realtor, Gwen Broughton, and humbly asked, "Do you work with people like us? People that need a little time to get our down payment together and qualify for the home?" Gwen held our hand throughout the process. On May 15, 1992, three weeks after our second son was born, our American Dream of homeownership became a reality.

This backstory is the driving force behind this book and my entire career in the insurance industry. Thirty years later, I still think about this younger version of myself. How badly I wanted to own a home and how little I knew about the process of homeownership. I won't bore you with the details of how hard we worked to come up with the down payment. What I will tell you is that my passion for excellence and expertise is fueled by your backstory. The path to home ownership is paved with obstacles that each buyer must overcome. Insurance is just one of those hurdles.

This book will clearly articulate WHY you need to take your homeowner's insurance policy very seriously. It will address the two words I hate the most in my industry:

"Cheap Insurance." It will answer the question that you are thinking about right now: How do I choose the right agent, agency, or company to protect my most valuable assets? There are certain professional relationships that you would not consider changing no matter what. Maybe that includes your beautician/barber, doctor, dentist, maybe your favorite restaurant, your CPA, tax preparer, or lawyer might make the list as well. I will argue that as a homeowner, you need a personal relationship with your insurance agent/agency.

I will share clear and vivid stories on the importance of each key coverage category in your policy. Not only will I talk about what you are covered for. I will TELL THE TRUTH about what is not covered in any insurance policy, regardless of the company or carrier. Along that same line, I will give out clear direction on when you should and should not file a claim. The example that I like to share is that if a kid accidentally breaks your window with a baseball, is it covered? The answer is yes. The better question is: Should you file a claim since it is covered? If the cost to repair the window is less than or slightly higher than your deductible, the answer is no.

Spoiler alert. Does your current home insurance company contact you annually and offer a complete policy review? If not, get out! Seriously, stop reading and call my agency right now, and we will give you the level of service that you deserve. Is your home the same today as it was the day that you moved in? No. You have made changes, and you may have changed as well. Your job? Your family?

INTRODUCTION

Your assets? Any renovations or home improvements? Any nice new jewelry or perhaps a Rolex watch that needs to be scheduled on your policy as a rider?

Breaking news. Your current home insurance policy does not cover you in the event of a flood, and your policy will not pay off the mortgage in the event of your death or disability. Sorry, I just like telling the God's honest truth. It is much easier than leading you on to sell a policy today but leaving you gravely disappointed when a natural disaster shows up. You need to know the truth. And more importantly, you need to know that you can purchase other insurance policies to be properly protected. *The Property Insurance B.I.B.L.E. is your personal guide to getting* **Better Home Insurance Before Losing Everything.**

CHAPTER 1

The Dream of Homeownership

"Life can change in a minute. One minute you can be enjoying your beautiful home, and the next minute you can be sued for the value of your home"

- Kevin Spann

Before we get too heavy into protecting your assets with the right kind of homeowner's insurance, I think we should spend time talking about becoming a homeowner. Some would argue that becoming a homeowner is the epitome of the American Dream. Others would counter that homeownership is a pipe dream that most people cannot even afford to think about. What is the point of dreaming about something that is as probable as taking a shuttle flight to planet Mars? And if the chance of buying a home is so far-fetched, why should anyone think about protecting this asset with homeowner's insurance?

Let's start with the American Dream. Will Smith's character (Chris Gardner) in the 2006 film, *The Pursuit of Happyness*, pondered this great question. He wondered why the founding fathers wrote about the "pursuit of happiness" versus happiness as being an American birthright. Was it because they knew that true happiness was unattainable?

The phrase "the American Dream" was coined in 1931 by writer James Truslow Adams in his book *Epic of America*. Why would he write about the American Dream two years after the Great Depression? Probably for the same reasons that I'm writing about protecting your assets with home ownership, two years after the COVID-19 pandemic. The dream is still alive and well.

Would you agree that homeownership fits within the scope of your material definition of the American Dream? I have always equated homeownership with the American Dream. White house. Picket fence. Maybe a PVC fence. A space and a place to become the best version of yourself.

Maybe your dream is a little different. Is it a beachfront property in Malibu, California? Is it a sprawling ranch tucked away neatly in the woods of rural Wake Forest, North Carolina? Maybe you see yourself in a luxury duplex on the Upper East Side of Manhattan.

Here is positive proof that the American Dream and the pursuit of homeownership is alive and well. Recently I listened to the *Strictly Free Game* podcast hosted by Shawn Waller, where his guest, Author, Speaker, and CEO, Matthew Garland, talked about selling over 12,000 copies of the *First Time Home Buyers Guide*. In the podcast, Matthew talked about his journey across urban areas throughout the country, speaking to large audiences about real estate, investments, and how to qualify for a mortgage. At the end of these well-attended events, he was often asked, "How do you buy a house? How do I get started?"

His homeowners' guide was published in 2021. That is one year, post pandemic and over 90 years after the American Dream phrase was coined. I rest my case.

Buying a home is arguably the largest purchase that most people will ever make in their life. In October 2021, a *Yahoo Finance* article noted that the median home price nationwide passed $400,000 for the first time ever. This was driven by several factors, including, but not limited to low interest rates, limited inventory, and bidding wars that drove prices even higher.

Aspiring homeowners do whatever it takes to navigate the home buying process. Whether it's working more hours, getting a second or third job, cleaning up credit, or committing to a very aggressive savings plan. When the goal is to own a home, people dig deep to make it happen. I am often moved by the stories I hear when speaking at First Time Home Buying Seminars. When the idea of home ownership gets real, people will move heaven and earth to get there.

A friend and client shared a story of going to a home buying seminar at a local church. They introduced him to a one-year program that gave him guidance on credit, saving money, and qualifying for affordable housing grants. He wasn't a member of the church, but he attended the weekly program religiously. My client learned things he had never been introduced or exposed to growing up in an underprivileged area where financial literacy was not a common conversation.

He worked hard and saved harder and increased his credit score (which by the way he did not know that anyone was keeping) from sub-500, to a very respectable 700 plus. He took on a second job and saved every dime to meet the down payment required. A year and half after starting this journey, he was the proud owner of a high-ranch home with a sizable backyard for his kids to enjoy.

As he shared his journey, I kept thinking about how important it was that I properly insure his property. This was not a random transaction—this was personal. Of course, it is important to explore the most affordable home insurance option, but more importantly, I had to ensure that he and his family were properly protected from disasters, catastrophes, and any other sudden and accidental events that could ruin his dream. It has been several years since I wrote that policy, and he has never filed a single claim. We review his policy every year and update his coverages to keep up with the various home improvements that he has made.

Let's start with "why." When your why is big enough, you will find the how. Why did you pick this book up? Are you a current homeowner? Are you an aspiring homeowner? What's your backstory? Can you relate to my client who picked up the second job and did what he had to do to save every dollar and clean up his credit?

Behind every home, there is an incredible why. As an insurance agent, I get to hear these stories all day, every day, and I draw great inspiration from my clients.

My agency is based in Middle Village (Queens), New York. Queens has been called the most diverse county in America. Almost half of Queens' residents are born outside the United States, and over one hundred languages are spoken in this county. My agency is centrally located, smack in the middle of this melting pot. I get to share the joy of first generation and second-generation families that achieve the dream of homeownership. I also get to share the pain when there is a fire, flood, or some other awful act that threatens to steal or destroy what they worked their whole life to achieve.

Imagine this: You have worked hard and purchased your dream home. When you bought your house twenty years ago for $200,000, you never imagined that your home value would increase to over $1,000,000. You are still the same person. Hardworking, blue-collar job, working for New York City MTA or Corrections, or the Housing Authority. The neighbors love you because your property is always well maintained. And then one day there is a knock at your door. You open it and to your surprise you are being sued because someone said they slipped and fell because you did not shovel or salt the ice on your sidewalk. Now what?

Recently, this happened to one of my clients. He called me, very upset because he was being sued. Why? The letter stated that someone slipped and fell on the ice in front of his house. It came from a lawyer which gave him even greater concern.

Fortunately, I have completed several annual policy reviews with this client and always advised, "If you're ever sued, just call me." Your home insurance policy comes with an attorney. If you are ever sued for any personal liability matter, we will defend you. More importantly, if we lose, we will pay up to the liability limits on your policy.

This gave him some peace of mind. We kept talking, and I shared having similar experiences with other clients and explained that a letter is not a subpoena, which simply means that being accused didn't require him to respond or take any other action. After completely calming him down, we discussed the date on the letter. A quick Google search revealed that there was no snow, ice, or other weather-related event that would have made his sidewalk slippery.

Some days I sell insurance. Other days I give "assurance" that everything will be okay. The letter turned out to be a false attempt to scare my client out of his hard-earned money. The key point is that life can change in a minute. One minute you can be enjoying your beautiful home, and the next minute you can be sued for the value of your home.

The ultimate purpose of home insurance is to protect your most valuable asset from accidents, natural disasters, catastrophes, and lawsuits. I opened this chapter with the quote "Dreams don't work unless you do: It was all a dream," by noted author, John C. Maxwell. I talked about the pursuit of happiness and the origin of the phrase "The American Dream." Also, I reinforced that the American Dream is alive and well, based on the overwhelming response to Matthew Garland's, *The Home Buying Process* in 2021. Examples were given of one man's year-long pursuit to buy a house, and I also detailed how quickly your dream house can be lost with a frivolous lawsuit. Ultimately, this is why it is so important to properly protect your asset with both the right home insurance coverage and a personal relationship with an insurance agent or agency that can guide you along the way.

> **Key Take aways**
>
> - The dream of homeownership is alive and well.
> - People will do whatever it takes to achieve the dream of homeownership.
> - The 2021 median price of a home in the United States was $400,000.
> - Homeowners should have a relationship with a personal insurance agent or agency that can help them protect their home from accidents, natural disasters, catastrophes, and lawsuits.

CHAPTER 2

The Choice is Yours

> *"Choosing the right home insurance agent and/or agency to provide homeowner's insurance requires the same due diligence that you put into finding your house"*
> *- Kevin Spann*

How do you choose the right insurance agent or insurance agency to insure your home? This is a serious question that merits time and debate. You have worked hard to buy a house. You are going to close on the home within seven to ten business days, and your realtor and lender have advised that this is the last step in the home buying process. The bank requires that you secure a home insurance policy listing them as the lienholder. Once this process is complete, your closing date will be set, and you and your loved ones can take possession of your dream home.

This sounds simple enough. Heck, it is 2022. You have a smartphone or tablet in your hand. A quick Google search for "home insurance" should do it, right?

I did the search for you, and here are the top five responses:

- GEICO for your Home – Get a Free Quote in Minutes
- Compare Top 10 Home Insurance – Find Your Best Rate in Minutes
- 10 Best Homeowners Insurance – Cheapest Rates in 2 minutes
- Get A Home Insurance Quote/Allstate
- Compare Home Insurance Quotes: Get the Best Rates (2022)

This is pretty easy. All you have to do is click on the hyperlink(s), and you will have the best rates and "cheap" insurance to protect perhaps the largest asset that you have ever purchased in your life.

How does that make you feel? Think about your personal journey to homeownership. All the time you invested in finding an affordable property in the safest neighborhood, with the best school district that your money could buy. When you started to look for a house, did you do it all yourself, or did you work with a team of professional advisors? Did you buy the home with the help of a realtor, or did you do it on your own? How did you finance your home? Did you get a loan from your primary bank or credit union? Did you work with a mortgage broker or lender who got to know you and your unique situation? What about the appraiser, home inspector, attorney, and all the other professional services that you utilized during the home buying process? Did you choose any of these services with a Google search or personal recommendations?

Choosing the right home insurance agent and/or agency to provide homeowner's insurance requires the same due diligence. You want a qualified professional that will help you find the best coverage at the best rate. Buying a home insurance policy is not just a transaction, it is the beginning of a long-term relationship. Let's do a quick checklist of factors that you want to consider:

- Are they knowledgeable?
- Are they available?
- Are they reputable?
- Does the price include personal advice?
- Can they discuss all the key policy coverages in simple terms?
- Will they offer an annual review of your policy?
- Will the policy be customized to your unique needs?
- Are they honest and transparent about what is not covered by your policy?

Let's start with how you identify a knowledgeable insurance agent. A well-versed agent should be able to discuss the six key coverages that are included in all Homeowner Insurance policies. How can you tell if the agent you are dealing with is well informed? He or she should ask more questions than they give answers. That is it. Simple questions like, Will you be living in this house as your primary residence? Or, is this an investment property that you are buying to rent out to others? Let's stop right there. By definition, a "homeowners" insurance policy is for a home that is occupied by the homeowner. Real estate investors reading this should be very concerned. "I own several rental properties; you mean I'm not covered?" Absolutely. Rental properties should be covered by a Landlord's Package policy. It will cost a few more dollars to insure the property, but your investment will be properly protected.

What else? A knowledgeable insurance agent should ask you several questions about your personal finances to make sure your assets are properly protected. Tell me about what you do for a living. Do you own any other properties?

Coverage E is the Comprehensive Personal Liability coverage on a home insurance policy. We live in a world where people love to sue. Who is more likely to be sued? A doctor? A lawyer? A police officer? A well-known athlete or entertainer? The millionaire next door who built their fortune as a tradesman, but also invested slowly and consistently in the market? All of the above. A good insurance agent will ask (God forbid): If you were sued, how much would a good lawyer come after you for? Based on the answer to that question, he or she will recommend the proper amount of liability insurance to protect you personally.

Many people are credited with the quote, "Availability is your best ability." Can you contact your agent or a licensed professional or their team anytime? Natural disasters happen at any time. Is your agent available by cell phone or text in the event of an emergency? Do they have a strong digital presence across all social media platforms? If the power goes out, which is happening once or twice a year throughout the country, can you still get in touch with your agency?

Let me pause to distinguish between an agent, an agency, and an insurance company. Most insurance companies have a website and a 1-800 number that consumers can call seven days a week, twenty-four hours a day. However, you will never speak with the same person twice. How do I know? Ask the representative for their direct line and can you deal with them personally if you ever have a billing issue or claim question. The answer will be no.

Conversely, I'm using the words "agent" and "agency" interchangeably. A local agency is generally very knowledgeable of the common risks that impact their area. They usually have a staff of licensed professionals that you will build a strong personal relationship with over a period of time. They are likely to be involved in the local community and are easily accessible if you have questions.

Full disclosure—I am very biased toward doing business with a local agent. Personally, I think there is tremendous value in personal service for all things at all times. I use technology as much as the next person, however, when it comes to major purchases and professional advice, I am always going to choose personal service.

Here is another advantage of receiving personal service from your homeowner's insurance agent. What if a windstorm comes along and rips the siding on your house? Should you file a claim? An insurance agency can give you the proper advice. They will most likely ask you to get an estimate of the damage. Next, they will discuss your deductible and if it makes good financial sense to file a claim. If the damage is less than the deductible, the homeowner is better off repairing or replacing the siding themselves. This protects their premium for the long run and saves the insurance policy for major events.

Is the insurance agency reputable? If they are being recommended by your family, friends, co-worker, realtor, or lender, I would say yes. They have done something right to earn their trust and referral. Another way to determine reputation is by online reviews. What do other clients say about their service? Start with the idea that nobody is perfect. That being said, I wouldn't limit myself to only doing business with agents that have perfect 5-star reviews. I would choose the agency the same way we choose hotels and restaurants these days. How do they respond to unfavorable reviews? Also, what does their digital and social media presence say about the agency? Do you share any similar community causes? Are they helping the fight against cancer? Do they support local youth sports?

A good agency should be able to discuss key coverages without sounding like they are reading from a script. They should ask you for a detailed description of your house, and then be able to explain how your house (dwelling) is covered by Coverage A. They should ask you to tell them about everything that is on your property. If that description includes anything like a shed, detached garage, etc., they should be able to tell you how much is allotted for Coverage B or other structure coverage that you have.

The same goes for your Personal Property Protection (Coverage C). I always go with the "dumping the Barbie house" description here. If you can imagine holding your house upside down, and everything that falls out is covered under Coverage C. Have the agent clarify whether you're covered on a Full Replacement Cost basis or an Actual Cash Value basis. This is something you want to know long before you ever have a claim.

The last few things to look for when choosing an insurance agency are equally important as everything I have laid out thus far. First, does this policy come with an annual review? Are they going to reach out to you every year to make sure your policy is keeping up with the other changes in your life? If the answer is no, run. Thank me later. I've been doing this for a very long time. It makes me sick to my stomach every time I ask someone who their house is insured with, and they don't know. I don't blame the client. I blame the company for being lazy and not reaching out to the client consistently. More on that in our chapter that is dedicated to the importance of the annual review.

No two people are the same. No two households are the same. That being said, no two insurance policies should be the same. Every policy must be customized to fit the unique needs of the policyholder. The only way to customize a policy is to ask personal questions and be comfortable with every answer. Questions such as, "Are you the only one on the deed" will open up a great dialogue and help you get to know your client. People that buy property together, regardless of race, religion, gender, sexual preference, or relationship, have the right to be listed on the policy. They have the full rights to the policy of the named insured and deserve to be treated with the same level of dignity and respect. This is especially important as loved ones pass on and transition. Properly listing everyone on the policy will ensure a smooth transition of the home insurance policy to the rightful named insured.

Here is a game changer question. Ask the insurance agency, "Is there anything that's not covered on my policy?" If they do not quickly say, "Yes. Flood Insurance is not included in any home insurance policy, and this policy does not include life insurance protection to pay off the mortgage if the policyholder passes away." Any other answer is not right and unacceptable. If they do not know this, you have to question and doubt what else they do not know.

Noted speaker and leader, Dr. Myles Munroe said, "Our life is the sum total of all the decisions we make every day, and those decisions are determined by our priorities." Many people mistakenly think they do not have any choices when it comes to their home insurance. If I had a dollar for every time I was told: "You can't change your home insurance because it's with the bank." I would be a much wealthier man. The truth is, the choice is yours. You can change your home insurance at any time. You simply have to make it a priority.

Key Take aways

1. How to choose an insurance agency.
2. Look for a knowledgeable agency that can customize the policy to fit your needs.
3. Is the agency available to do business the way you want? Call? Text? E-mail? Social media?
4. Check online reviews to see if the agency is reputable.
5. Does price include advice?
6. Will the agency reach out and offer an annual review?
7. Are they able to clearly explain what is not covered?

CHAPTER 3

The Value of a Great Relationship

> *"All good relationships are built over time.*
> *The relationship with your insurance*
> *agent should start with getting you*
> *the best coverage at the best rate"*
>
> *- Kevin Spann*

Think about all the people you do business with today. Not the random online transactions or the Amazon delivery person that stops by a couple of times a week. I mean the personal business relationships you have with people that you know and trust. Think about the rapport you have built with your barber or beautician. Is your conversation limited to the exact style, cut, and color you want for your hair this week? Or do you discuss things at a deeper level?

Quick exercise challenge. Grab a sheet of paper and pen. Or feel free to take notes on your phone, tablet, or Remarkable notepad (I am currently learning how to use this). Take one minute to write down the key business relationships that you have. How many names did you come up with? Who made your list? What is so special about that business that you only work with that person and not their competitors?

Full disclosure. I did the exercise as well and came up with ten businesses. My doctor, dentist, barber, lawyer, local deli, gas station, photographer, electrician, car salesman, electrician, and landscaper. Why the local deli? Because Lou remembers exactly how I want my coffee prepared: medium hot coffee, half and half, no sugar. Why the electrician? Because I went to school with Rodney. He has wired my business, my home, and taken great care of everybody in my family that I have referred to him over the past twenty-five years. Why the local gas station? Because they still provide full service at the same price that other stations charge, but you do not have to get out of the car and pump the gas yourself.

Be honest with me. Did your insurance agent make the list? I would argue that the value of the relationship with your personal insurance agent should easily be on your top ten. The depth of the relationship with your insurance agent should go deeper than the price, but also include the quality and quantity of advice they offer. After all, when you choose an agent to insure your home, you are choosing someone to protect what is likely your most valuable asset.

All good relationships are built over time. The relationship with your insurance agent should start with getting you the best coverage at the best rate. Very similar to the realtor, the agent should have intimate knowledge of the local area. Let's say your home is located in an area that is prone to flooding or water backing up through the sewer system. Wouldn't you want an agent that could recommend the right coverage before you need it?

One of the greatest values of having a personal bond with your insurance agent is that they will customize a policy just for you. The six key coverages on a home insurance policy are defined the same way for all insurance carriers. The thing that distinguishes one agent from another agent or one company from another company, is how they get to know their client and build a policy that is tailor-made for that person.

Let's start with the coverage conversation. The key coverages are the same for all carriers. There's Coverage A—the dwelling coverage to repair or replace your home. There is Coverage B or Other Structures Protection. This covers any additional structures on your property such as a detached garage, shed, gazebo, etc. While gathering information to insure your home, a good agent will build a rapport and ask open-ended questions: "Tell me about your house." The reply to this statement will reveal details that will help insure the home properly. "It has a new roof." Great, we offer a new roof discount. I will add that to your policy. "It has a finished basement." Wonderful. We should talk about water backup coverage to protect this area.

Personal property is protected under Coverage C. It is generally set to a formula of seventy percent of the dwelling coverage. An important question that a good local agent will ask is: "Other than the traditional items we find in most homes, are there any specialty items that you collect?"

Whether the homeowner collects art, stamps, memorabilia, baseball cards, or fine silverware is not important. The key here is that you are getting to know your client, and the homeowner is getting to know you. We will talk more about the special riders and endorsements for collectibles later in the book.

Additional Living Expenses (ALE) or Loss of Use is the coverage that will pay to put you and your family in a hotel if your home can't be occupied due to a covered loss. No two families are the same, therefore, you cannot take a cookie cutter approach to this coverage. Here is a story to illustrate this point.

A good friend and long-term client of mine had an electrical fire in her home in the fall of 2020. A power surge in the electric panel made the home uninhabitable until the local power company agreed that the home was safe to live in. Her family included her ninety-year-old mother, two children, and three school-age grandchildren.

In normal times, it is a challenge for family and friends to open their doors and accommodate a family of six. At the height of the Covid-19 pandemic, social distancing, remote schooling, and remote work made it even more challenging. Her mother needed accommodations for her oxygen tank and other medical needs. The grandchildren needed space and high-powered wireless access to do their homework and keep up in school. Working remotely also required space and unlimited wi-fi.

Fortunately, I knew the family and made sure they had robust ALE coverage. Not only did we pay the expense of multiple rooms at a quality hotel. We also cut a check to pay for their meals and other expenses they incurred. Feeding a family of six is costly. Feeding a family of six, eating out three times a day—for a week—will do serious damage to your budget!

Most claims happen outside of normal business hours. This was no different. It happened around 10:00 p.m. Everyone made it out safely and checked in the hotel to get a good night's sleep. When we spoke the next morning, I reminded her of what was included in her ALE coverage. Secondly, I reached out to our claims department and had them cut a check for food. Our claims department also contacted the hotel, took ownership of the bill, and made the family much more comfortable in multiple rooms. This is the value of a relationship with your insurance agent. It is much better than buying from a 1-800 number where you will never speak to the same person twice. And forget the idea of a personal relationship!

"What do you do for a living?" Here is another great question that can *show* the value of having a relationship with your insurance agent. In this lawsuit-crazy world that we live in, your agent can *prove his or her worth* just by asking this question.

All home insurance policies come with Coverage E or Personal/Family Liability protection. This coverage protects you in the event of a lawsuit. A good local agent will recommend liability limits that align with your assets.

Also, local insurance agents are often involved in the local community. This makes the agent a very resourceful person for the first-time homebuyer, or the person that is moving into a new neighborhood. Beyond selling you a policy, he or she is probably a great resource when it comes to recommending local contractors should you have a claim, or simply want to make improvements on your home.

Buying a home insurance policy should not be viewed as a one-time transaction. Oftentimes, I will have conversations with young couples and first-time homebuyers about riders, endorsements, and coverage that they should purchase. However, we're always cognizant that the homebuyer needs to stay within a certain debt-to-income ratio to get through closing. Realtors and lenders love referring clients to our agency because we understand their business as well.

Annual policy reviews are the unique value proposition of our agency. We proactively reach out to our clients at every renewal to make sure their policy is keeping up with their lifestyle.

When we first write a policy, we always inform the policyholder of certain policy limitations, such as: jewelry is only covered for one-thousand dollars per item. Additional jewelry coverage can be purchased as a rider on the home insurance policy, or in a separate policy with a carrier such as Jewelers Mutual. Whatever and whenever the client buys the extra coverage is up to them.

We never know which clients will respond to the multiple communication efforts we make to schedule an annual review. We mail, e-mail, call, and (with client's permission) text to remind our insureds that it is time to schedule an annual review. New policy coverages and new policy discounts are being updated all the time. In 2022, my primary carrier introduced "Service Line Coverage," which will cover the cost of damage to the pipes that lead from the home to the street.

My best and worst story on the benefits of an annual review are both the same. We had a lovely couple in the office for an annual review. We noticed the beautiful bling-bling on her wedding finger and suggested they schedule the ring on the policy. They agreed and scheduled the 2.8 carat, diamond cut, oval ring (a tenth-year anniversary present) on the policy.

A few years later, this same couple returned to the office in tears. She lost the ring down the drain while washing dishes. She was obviously very emotional and wanted to find out if there was any coverage. I felt bad for her loss, but I felt great when I checked her records and reminded her that she was in good hands! The $32,000 ring was replaced, and she has continuously shown her gratitude by referring numerous clients to us over the years.

Key Take aways

1. Take a minute to write down the business relationships that you value the most and why.
2. All good relationships are built over time.
3. Building a relationship with your insurance agent adds value.
4. Home insurance should be customized to meet your needs.
5. Are your current liability limits aligned with your assets?
6. Is your agent resourceful beyond selling you an insurance policy?
7. An Annual Review is the Unique Value Proposition of my agency. Does your policy come with an annual review?

CHAPTER 4

Home is Where the Heart is

> *"When I think of home, I think of all the right kinds of property insurance to protect it."*
> — *Kevin Spann*

If someone were to invite you to their home, what kind of home do you immediately visualize? Your vision is undoubtedly influenced by where the person lives. If they live in the suburbs, you might imagine that they live in a single-family home. If they live in a city or more urban area, you might think of their home as an apartment within a multi-family house or a large apartment complex. There is no right or wrong answer. People in cities, suburbs, and rural areas all have their own idea of a "home." I think Dorothy said it best in the theme song from "The Wizard of Oz."

Everyone is familiar with the song, "Home." It was first made famous by the well-known play and movie, *The Wizard of Oz*. Its life span was extended by the Stephanie Mills version from *The Wiz*. And if either of these renditions have escaped you, someone has attempted to sing the song in every local high school talent show. *American Idol, Live at the Apollo,* and a host of other television shows have also served as a platform for contestants to belt out their best version of "Home."

Just like the song "Home," there are several versions of Home Insurance. No two people think of the same image when they think of home. People who rent apartments refer to their apartment as "home." Shareholders who own co-op apartments refer to their unit as "home." Condo owners refer to their unit as a "home," whether it is in a Manhattan skyscraper or a standalone dwelling in any part of the country. Suburbanites who own single-family dwellings consider their ranch or colonial-style dwelling to be home. On the contrary, real estate investors who own two-family dwellings or multi-family properties often *mistakenly* insure investment properties on a *home* insurance policy.

Insurance companies and state insurance departments are clear on their definitions of various types of home insurance. Consumers, however, are in the dark. The average Joe does not know that if they choose the wrong type of home insurance *they* are not covered. It sounds cold, but it is true and simple. You can pay a significant premium on a policy for years and make the mistake of thinking that you are fully covered.

Think about your first apartment. Was it a studio? One bedroom? Two bedrooms? Our first apartment was a two-bedroom garden apartment in Islip, New York. This was a major step-up from the master bedroom my wife, newborn son, and I shared at my mother-in-law's house. Money was tight so we furnished one room at a time, one dollar at a time.

The sofa and loveseat came from Sears Outlet ($200). The kitchen set, glass table with four matching chairs were purchased at Job Lot or Odd Lot. We financed the $1,500 master bedroom set from Levitz Furniture, my former employer. I do not remember how much my son's captain bed or the stereo system or the twenty-five-inch floor-model television cost, but in 1987 we had our first place, and every room was filled with our stuff.

At the time, I had never heard of renters insurance. Hence, I did not have any. Unlike home insurance, it was not mandatory. When you add the cost of my furniture and appliances, we had a few thousand dollars of "stuff." Add in our clothing, shoes, and other miscellaneous things that people take for granted, like bedding, sheets, pots, pans, etc., we had more personal property than we imagined. Thank God we never had a fire or theft, as it would have caused a devastating financial setback.

Fast forward to today, and I see myself and my wife in young couples that I insure. Everyone pays a significant premium for car insurance in New York. One of the ways I encourage people to reduce the cost of their car insurance is by bundling it with renters insurance. Believe it or not, it is less expensive to have car insurance and renters insurance, than to have car insurance by itself. Not only does this strategy save my clients money; it also protects them against unforeseen claims.

Here is my best example to illustrate this point. One Saturday night in March 2019, after a full day of watching college basketball, I turned on the 11:00 news. The breaking story showed a devastating fire at Avalon Courts in Melville, New York, about ten minutes from my home. I recognized the name of the person being interviewed by the reporter. It was one of my clients, Jennifer P. I quickly pulled out my laptop and confirmed that it was her. More importantly, I verified that her renter's insurance policy was still active. It was–thank God. I called Jennifer at 11:30 p.m. and told her she was "in Good Hands," and I would be there to see her first thing in the morning.

Jennifer's first floor apartment was destroyed by a fire that started on the second floor. I met Jennifer and several of her neighbors in the parking lot and observed the devastation. Several units were roped off with yellow tape and police barricades. The roofs from this recently built townhouse-like community were destroyed. Neighboring apartments were boarded up and uninhabitable because of the water and smoke damage.

Jennifer's policy cost less than fifteen dollars a month and offered incredible benefits. The Additional Living Expenses (ALE) coverage paid for Jennifer, her husband, and toddler to stay in a hotel for up to a year. This gave them great peace of mind. Families can make it through anything as long as they can stay together. Jennifer laughed as she remembered only buying this policy because of my recommendation to bundle and save.

Some of Jennifer's neighbors were not so lucky. I was the only insurance company representative there. Several people pulled their policy up on their phones and asked for my guidance. Sadly, one of the largest carriers only offered $7,000 for Loss of Use or Additional Living Expenses. That was only enough to cover a couple of weeks of hotel, meals, and other expenses at best. Needless to say, quite a few of those neighbors are now my clients.

For the past fifteen years, I have been a frequent speaker at co-op and condo association meetings throughout the downstate New York area. I have helped many associations implement mandatory insurance programs to help their cooperators and shareholders better protect their assets. While attending these meetings, I often learn much more than I teach. As with every other kind of "home" insurance that is discussed in this book, it always starts with why. "Why do I need insurance for my unit? The building already has insurance." Correct and correct. All condos and co-ops have a Master Policy that covers the building and common areas. However, the master policy does not include any coverage for the shareholder or unit owner's personal belongings, building property, personal liability, loss of use, or a host of other perils. Condo insurance is incredibly reasonable as it can be purchased for as little as ten to fifteen dollars per month on the low-end, or for several thousand dollars a year depending on which assets need to be protected.

I love the economic diversity of New York City. Whether I'm speaking in a Mitchell Lama affordable cooperative unit to shareholders with moderate or fixed income, or to the wealthy clients on the Upper East Side, the conversation is always the same. The reason you need a personal condo or co-op insurance policy is to protect your personal property against unforeseen fires, water damage, smoke, theft, and a host of other perils, very similar to renters insurance.

However, there are key additional coverages that go above and beyond what is included in a renters policy. Building Property Protection (BPP) and Loss Assessments are two of the most common coverages. BPP coverage protects any improvements and betterments that an owner makes to his or her unit. If someone invests thousands of dollars to upgrade their kitchen or bathroom, they should obtain an equal amount of BPP coverage to protect their investment.

Earlier I mentioned that all associations carry a Master Policy which protects the replacement cost of the building and liability exposure in common areas. However, if a building sustains a loss that is greater than the policy coverage, the Master Policy includes a provision to assess all shareholders/owners for their portion of the loss. This is better known as "Loss Assessment" coverage. One of my insureds was assessed $11,000 after a significant fire and water loss took place in his building. He was extremely happy when we shared that his policy had $25,000 of Loss Assessment protection, and he would not have to worry about spending a dime out of his personal finances. Are you in a financial position to write a check for $11,000 if your policy does not have enough loss assessment coverage?

The first thing that distinguishes a Homeowners policy from a Renters Insurance policy or a Condo policy is Coverage A, or the dwelling protection coverage. This coverage will pay to replace your home if the *house* is *totally* destroyed, and it needs to be repaired, rebuilt, or renovated from damage caused by a covered peril. Further, it comes with Coverage B, or other structure protection, which covers any additional structures on the property that are not attached to the house. This includes a detached garage, shed, playground, deck, and a host of other backyard fixtures that you can imagine.

No one plans to file a home insurance claim, but things happen. The most important thing is that the dwelling coverage listed on the policy keeps pace with the true replacement cost of the property. Most carriers conduct an exterior inspection on new home insurance policies to make sure the coverage aligns with the actual cost to rebuild a house in the event of a total loss. However, homeowners renovate and upgrade their homes all the time. Think about this for a minute. What improvements have you made to your house since you moved in? First-time homebuyers, what changes do you plan to make as soon as your funds catch up with your goals and dreams? Realtors, have you ever listed a property that has not improved since purchase? Realtors, again, have you ever sold a home where there was no conversation about future enhancements?

Home renovation was a form of therapy during the pandemic! People were confined to their homes, working remotely, socially distancing, and trying to survive. They found peace and comfort in finishing basements, converting a bedroom to an office, or adding a sunroom with a Jacuzzi to better enjoy their personal space. Did anyone think of calling their insurance company to mention these changes and upgrade their policy? Did your insurance carrier/agent reach out to you in the past few years to review your policy?

The number one service that separates my agency from all other agencies and other carriers, is that we offer a consistent annual review process. I'll be brief here as a later chapter is fully dedicated to this subject. Let's say that your home is currently insured for $300,000. This coverage is based on the replacement cost of when you bought your home ten years ago. In the past few years, you invested $20,000 into your bathroom, $30,000 to upgrade your kitchen, and $50,000 to finish your basement. Your replacement cost is now $400,000, and your market value is significantly more!

And then, life shows up. You have a sudden and accidental loss; your home needs to be rebuilt from the ground up. On top of the emotional devastation, you contact your carrier and learn that your home is grossly underinsured. Who would you call? Do you know the name of your insurance carrier? Do you have a personal relationship with a local insurance agent? Have they ever contacted you to review your policy? I know—call the bank! The premium for your home insurance comes out of your mortgage, so they should know what to do. Maybe the person who recommended that you sign up for the cheapest policy just to get through closing will be there for you. If this conversation makes you uncomfortable, the time to switch insurance agents is today. Buy a policy from an agency where the annual premium includes an annual review of your policy. Do not wait until you are in the middle of a storm to find better coverage and probably a better rate.

The next type of property insurance we will discuss is a Landlord Insurance Policy or a DP-3. DP-3 (Dwelling Protection) is the policy coverage we recommend to most landlords (people who own properties that they do not live in). Like home insurance, DP-3 policies include coverage for the primary home structure and any additional structures on the property. Unlike home insurance, landlord policies include coverage for loss of rental income. Personal property protection on a home insurance policy is usually 50% to 70% of the dwelling coverage. Personal property on a DP-3 policy is typically 10% of the dwelling coverage and is generally limited to major appliances that are owned by the landlord: stove, refrigerator, dishwasher, and all other common appliances.

Liability insurance is also included in a Landlords policy. This protects the property owner if tenants or guests are injured on the property and the landlord is sued. How much liability insurance do you need? Enough to protect your assets if a good lawyer tried to sue you for your entire net worth. Common liability limits are usually:

1. $100,000
2. $300,000
3. $500,000
4. $1,000,000

The cost difference between $100,000 and $1,000,000 can be as little as $100. If you can afford to pay more, pay for the extra protection and thank me later.

Is being protected for loss of rental income important? I think so. The reason investors buy rental property is to generate a consistent stream of passive income. If your tenants move out and stop paying rent because of a covered peril, wouldn't you want your rental income to keep coming in? This is the biggest reason why property investors should protect their assets with a DP-3 policy that includes the proper amount of loss of rental income coverage. How much rental income coverage should you get? Your loss of income coverage should match your rent roll as it will need to be verified in the event of a claim.

This all sounds good, but some of you are thinking, *Does a landlord's policy cost more than a home insurance policy?* Yes, on average you should expect to pay 20% to 30% more. This is the cost to be the boss, the cost of doing business. Factor the cost of the better insurance policy into your rent and keep it moving.

Does a landlord policy cover my tenants' personal property? Absolutely not. I consistently encourage all landlords to REQUIRE their tenants to carry a separate renters insurance policy. As noted in the beginning of this chapter, renters' policies can be purchased for as little as $10 a month. If your tenant can't or won't pay for the insurance, you know what to do next. This is the same tenant who thinks all landlords are independently wealthy and will replace all their belongings in the event of a fire or water loss. Do you want to be a hero, or do you want to share that risk with an insurance company?

Real estate investors often make the mistake of buying "home insurance" for an investment property. As investors, their primary focus is on the income that will be generated by this rental property, or the large profit that will be made from flipping a house. I applaud and respect the goals, as real estate always has been and probably always will be the greatest path to wealth in America. However, I caution all investors to make sure they have the right property insurance policy to protect their investments every step of the way.

Let's start with some basic *policy coverage* language. A home insurance policy requires the homeowner to occupy the property. If the homeowner vacates the property for thirty to sixty days, the policy is null and void.

A vacant home requires a vacant home insurance policy, which will cover your property for causes of loss like fire, theft, and water damage during the time the home will be vacant. This is one instance where having a relationship with an insurance agent is priceless. An investor can and should be able to tell the agent their exact intentions, and the agent should in turn be able to provide the right kind of policy.

Does a vacant home insurance policy cost more than a regular home insurance policy? Of course! You do not have to be in the insurance business to recognize the risks that come with an empty house. Have you ever heard the saying, "Don't be penny-wise and dollar foolish?" If the vacant home insurance policy costs $200 more a year to protect a $500,000 investment, does it make sense to spend a little more to be properly protected?

I have the pleasure of working with a group of smart real estate investors who value my professional advice and recommendations when it comes to insuring their investment properties. They buy homes that are being sold by family estates. These are properties inherited by adult children who have no interest in holding on to their childhood home after mom or dad passed away. After going through all the proper legal and probate channels, these properties are purchased, renovated, and resold for a sizable profit.

My role is to make sure the home is properly insured during the renovation phase. We always establish a timeline for how long the property will be vacant and how much the property needs to be insured for. Most importantly, we keep the lines of communication open and remain flexible to change.

When I think of home, I think of all the right kinds of property insurance to protect it. This chapter was a journey through several types of property insurance. We started with a Renters Insurance policy, advanced to a Condo/Co-op Insurance policy, and spent considerable time talking about key coverages in a Homeowners Insurance policy. Next, we did a comparison and contrast of homeowners insurance versus landlords insurance and why it is important to have the right kind of policy. Finally, we talked about vacant properties from the perspective of a real estate investor. However, any individual or family who inherits a home that is not immediately occupied, should pay attention to the details on how a vacant home insurance policy works.

Key Take aways

- Tenants should protect their current assets with an affordable Renters Insurance policy.
- Shareholders and Co-operators should protect their belongings with a Co-op or Condo Insurance policy.
- Homeowners policies include coverage to replace the Dwelling and any other structures on the property.
- Personal property is protected at 50% to 70% of the replacement cost of the dwelling coverage amount.
- Landlords should protect their property with a DP-3 policy.
- DP-3 policies include loss of rental income.
- Homes that are vacant for more than thirty days need a vacant insurance policy.

CHAPTER 5

Let's Talk About Claims

> *"Anything that can go wrong will go wrong, and at the worst possible time"*
> – Murphy's Law

Everybody buys home insurance because it is required, but very few people know how the policy actually works. Does the policy cover anything and everything that can go wrong in your house? What is the responsibility of the insured on a home insurance policy, and what is the responsibility of the insurance company? You know how your deductible works for your car insurance, but how does it work for your home insurance?

First-time homebuyers may recall writing a check for their annual home insurance premium, but do they recall being informed about how their policy actually works? It is fair to assume that your house is covered in the event of a fire or if you are robbed, but is there anything else that is included? How about the opposite question: What is excluded from your policy that you should be worried about?

Beyond what is included or excluded from your home insurance policy, several items on your policy have a limited amount of coverage. When you go online to www.FastCheapInsurance.com, do they ask about the value of your engagement or wedding ring? Would you be shocked to learn that it is pretty common for individual jewelry items to be only covered for a maximum of $1,000 to $2,500? If you look at the bling on your ear lobes, neck, wrists, and fingers, keep reading closely.

A home insurance policy comes with a declaration page that clearly articulates what is and is not covered on your policy. Fortunately, or unfortunately, most people have never been bored enough to ever read the policy. The first few pages read like a preparation for a test that you would hate to take! It starts with crystal clear definitions of who's who, what's what, and when you can and should file a claim.

Let's break the boredom and try a quick exercise. Grab a pen and piece of paper and take one minute to write down everything you think you are covered for. Yes, you can also take notes on your phone or tablet but play fair. Let's make the game interesting. Think of Steve Harvey's voice on the *Family Feud* ... are you there yet? And the category is, "Things you think your home insurance policy will cover." Go!

_____

_____

How much fun was that? What did you come up with? Fire? Of course. Theft? Obviously. Wind damage from a natural disaster? Yes and no. Flooding? Never!

In addition to owning and operating my insurance agencies, I'm also a Certified Continuing Education Instructor for Real Estate Professionals. I recently asked this same question in front of a group of aspiring realtors, and those are the exact answers that I received. Fire is a covered peril on all insurance policies. Theft or robbery is also covered, but the amount of coverage will vary. If your belongings are stolen directly from your place of residence, you are fully covered. However, if your personal property, such as a laptop or tablet, is stolen from your car, you are only covered for ten percent of your total Personal Property Protection amount. Damage caused by the wind is also covered, but wind damage often carries a separate and higher deductible. Lastly, damage caused by flooding is always excluded from all home insurance policies, but we will deal with that more in a later chapter.

Let's take a minute and talk about deductibles. A deductible is the portion of the claim that you (the insured) are responsible for. If you are looking for a way to save money on your home insurance, start with the deductible.

The higher the deductible on your policy, the lower the cost of insurance. The lower the deductible, the higher the cost of your home insurance.

Deductibles can be selected in increments of $250. Again, the deductible is the amount of the claim that you (the insured), are responsible for. It is not uncommon to see older insurance policies that were written in the 1970s or occasionally, the 1980s with a deductible of only $250. At the time, people may have had less disposable income and did not want to risk being on the hook for too much money if they ever had to file a claim.

Today, most peril deductibles start at $1,000. That means that you are responsible for the first $1,000 of any covered loss on your property. One of my respected competitors recently changed their deductible to one half percent of the dwelling coverage. In other words, if your home is covered for $500,000 your deductible is automatically set at $2,500. That can be an issue if you do not have adequate savings or cash set aside to repair your home if a bad weather event rips the shingles off your roof or the siding off your home. What is worse is if you had no knowledge that your deductible increased, and you did not find out until after you filed a small claim.

Here is an example we often share with clients and prospects to help them understand when they should and should not file a claim.

Question: "If a kid accidently hits a baseball and it breaks your kitchen window, is it covered?"

Answer: Yes, because it is a sudden and accidental event.

Better question: "A kid hit a baseball and broke my window. Should I file a claim?"

Better answer: "I would suggest getting an estimate to determine how much it costs to replace the window. If it is less than or only slightly more than your deductible, it is probably a good idea to fix it yourself and save your insurance for bigger events."

In our agency, the price comes with advice. We encourage our clients to call us before they file a claim so we can advise whether this situation is a good or bad claim to file. Filing a few minor claims in a short period of time can result in a significant increase to your policy premium or even worse, your policy can be non-renewed or canceled. Here is a recent story to illustrate this point.

A good friend of mine had a long-term relationship with a very reputable company. He was happy with the policy and its annual premium. And then, he got the dreaded non-renewal letter. "Your policy will not be renewed this year because of the 'recent claims activity' on your policy." How did they define recent? A water damage claim in 2021 and a wind claim from Hurricane Sandy in 2012! I know, that was ten years ago! How can a natural disaster claim from ten years ago be held against a customer now?

Fortunately, we were able to offer him and his family much better coverage at a much better rate. We did not hold the claims from ten years ago against him. Not only did we give them a better home insurance policy, but we also bundled their car insurance and saved them over $1,000 on their annual insurance premiums. Needless to say, this family was very happy, and they continue to flood our agency with family and friends that we can help just like them.

I wish this was an isolated incident, but it is not. New clients often come to us because they have been kicked out by a prior carrier, and the bank has "force-placed" them with a much more expensive policy. That being said, if you are a current homeowner and ever had a claim on your policy, the time to shop for new insurance is now. Why? Because the next claim might be the last claim.

Water damage is the most common type of claim on all property insurance policies. The average cost of water damage claims is in the ballpark of $5,000. Why water, and what kinds of claims am I talking about?

First, water is no respecter of people or property. The earth is two-thirds water and only one-third land. Water goes wherever it wants to go whenever it wants to go there. Water damage claims come from a variety of sources. A heavy rain coupled with strong winds can rip the roof off a home, and the water shows up like an unwanted house guest. Freezing pipes in the winter can burst and cause all kinds of havoc to your floors, furniture, and drywall. Water backing up through your sewer system and entering your home through the tub, shower, or toilet, can create both an ugly and smelly situation!

Let's take these three water damage examples and talk about what is covered, what is debatable, and what is not covered. Again, our general rule of thumb is "whatever is sudden and accidental" is covered. Whatever is the result of wear and tear or poor maintenance on your home is not covered.

A few years ago, I noticed water spots on my dining room ceiling. Being in the business, I knew that meant it was time to repair or replace my roof. A typical asphalt roof is designed to last ten to twenty years. Maintaining, repairing, and replacing the roof is the homeowner's responsibility. If I waited for a natural disaster to file a claim, an experienced claims adjuster would visit my home and immediately recognize the rotted wood, water spots on my walls, and probably determine that damage was the result of my neglect.

However, if someone had a relatively new roof, no water spots or rotted wood, the claim would be covered. The insurance company would cover all the costs to repair or replace the roof as well as any interior damage caused by the rain. Let's follow the logic and say the total damage was $5,000, and the client had a deductible of $1,000. The carrier would pay $4,000, and the balance would be the insured's responsibility.

Freezing temperatures can cause pipes to break and water to do all kinds of damage in your house. Think about where the pipes are located in your home. Now think which areas would get damaged if the pipes were to burst. This is an unlikely event as long as your house is heated at a comfortable 68 to 70 degrees. But what happens when a natural disaster causes a power outage for an extended period and the pipes burst? Now what? I will tell you what—you will have a mess on your hands, and you will need to file a claim.

Full disclosure, if the freezing pipes are a result of your negligence and not a covered peril, your coverage can be questioned, and your claim can be denied. What do you mean? How can this be my fault? If you are fortunate enough to be a snowbird, you must maintain the temperature in your primary home before leaving for your secondary home in a warmer climate. Many northerners bought winter homes south of the border over the past few years, and that is a beautiful thing! I hope to join this club in the very near future. Make sure you keep taking advantage of modern technology and regulating the temperature while enjoying life in Virginia Beach, Myrtle Beach, or Florida. A diligent claims adjuster will look back on recent heating and power bills to see if you maintained your home at the proper temperature before paying the claim.

Lastly, let's talk about water backup. Water backup is defined as water backing up into your home through the toilet, shower, or tub. This is a common occurrence in densely populated areas. My office is located in Queens, New York. It is one of the five New York City boroughs. For all the wonder and glory that New York City has to offer, the sewer system is not one of them. The New York City sewer system can only handle one inch of rain per hour. If heavy rains or a nor'easter hits the city faster than tourists going through midtown on New Year's Eve, the water will back up into your home.

Water backup is not a standard coverage on a home insurance policy. It is a rider that must be added. Here is where the value of a local agent really shows up. As a local insurance agent, I know which neighborhoods and more specifically, which blocks are most likely to get water backup damage. Fellow local agents across the country know their area better than any direct or online carrier that wouldn't know the difference between the Colorado Rockies or the coastal areas of Alabama, Louisiana, or Mississippi!

The cost of water backup coverage is nothing compared to the benefit and peace of mind you will have if you ever need to file a water backup claim. When Hurricane Ida ripped through Queens in September 2021, many basements and downstairs apartments were destroyed by water backup. Sadly, many of these people did not have water backup coverage and had to rely on FEMA loans to repair the damage done to their homes. That event is one of the driving forces behind why I am writing this book. The insurance industry owes you an explanation, and this book is just one of my efforts to provide it.

When I am not working, or speaking publicly about insurance, you can always find me in the digital space giving property insurance tips. Google me anywhere you go for social media content and listen to my podcasts everywhere. I recently recorded a sixty-second video and stressed the importance of people getting the maximum amount of water backup coverage available. Some carriers offer as little as $5,000 of water backup coverage, and other carriers offer a much more robust water backup coverage of up to $25,000.

Warning. If you have to ask your carrier about this coverage, what other coverages or discounts are you missing out on? The best time to find out if you are properly covered for water damage and a host of other coverages is today. The worst time to find out is right after you had a claim.

Key Take aways

1. Raising your deductible can lower the cost of home insurance.
2. The deductible is your responsibility. The insurance company is responsible for covered perils that exceed your deductible.
3. Did you play the one-minute coverage game? Any surprises?
4. Water is the most common cause of property damage, and the average claim is valued at $5,000.
5. Make sure you get the maximum amount of water backup coverage offered by your carrier.

CHAPTER 6

Natural Disasters

> *"When the storm hits, the time to prepare is over."*
> *— Kevin Spann*

Funny story alert.

I've been reciting this quote for years: "When it's time to perform, the time to prepare is over." It is undoubtedly something that I read or heard over the years that stuck with me. My sons have heard it a million times before a major sporting event or academic challenge. I have been reciting this quote for over twenty years to young men that I have coached in youth basketball. They have also heard it enough that they can finish the quote before I start. My weekly staff meetings always open with an inspirational or thought-provoking quote, and this one has made many appearances on my PowerPoint presentations.

I Googled the quote to give the true author the appropriate credit, as I should for the purposes of this book.

You will be shocked to learn what I found. After scrolling past a few modified versions of the quote, I found this:

Abraham Kevin Spann: Allstate Insurance – Plan. Prepare. Perform.

Plan.
Prepare.
Perform.

"When it's time to perform, the time to prepare is over." #preparation #opportunity #success #wallstreet #blackwallstreet #inspire #beinspired – Timeline photos - Jul 24, 2019.

This quote is extremely relevant to the subject of home insurance and the potential impact of natural disasters. Natural disasters are the natural enemy of homeowners. All the hard work. All the planning. All the preparation. All the savings to get the down payment to qualify for your mortgage. All the gifts you received at your housewarming party. All the renovations, improvements, and betterments that you made to your home over a lifetime of hard work and dedication, can be destroyed in one catastrophic weather-related event.

Quick exercise, before I dive too deep into the technical insurance aspects of this chapter. Grab your tablet, notes app on your phone, or a good old pen and sheet of paper. Write down the names of all the major storms that you remember in your lifetime. Be honest. Don't cheat, ask Siri, or use Google for help. Take one minute and one minute only, and let's see what you can come up with off the top of your head. Go!

I stopped writing and did the exercise as well. I set the timer on my phone, and this is my true list:

1. Sandy
2. Katrina
3. Gloria
4. Houston
5. Ida
6. Microburst
7. Haiti
8. California wildfires
9. Tsunami

Being in the insurance industry for thirty-five years, I honestly thought I would have a much longer list. Some of these hurricanes, tropical storms, and nor'easters impacted me and my geographic area personally. Hurricane Sandy (2011), Hurricane Ida (2021), Middle Village Microburst/Tornado (2010). Other natural disasters stayed with me because I remember being glued to the news and watching how it devastated other states, countries, and parts of the world that I have never been to. The endless videos of the people, property, and pets that are impacted by these events leave lasting impressions.

For the purposes of this book and home insurance, we will limit our discussion to what is covered and what is not covered on your home insurance policy. We will also expand upon our conversation about hurricane deductibles.

Let's start with a couple of words that define what is covered on your property insurance policy. A ***covered peril*** is a risk or cause of loss or event that your insurance company *will* pay for a claim unless it is specifically excluded from coverage. *The words 'covered peril" and its complicated meaning is exactly why you need a local insurance agent to simply explain what the heck you are covered for!*

According to an *independent insurance industry website,* www.PolicyGenius.com, "In homeowners insurance, a 'covered peril' is an event the insurance company ***agrees*** to reimburse you for should you file a claim. Covered perils include fire, lightning strikes, windstorms and hail, weight of snow and ice."

"Your homeowner's insurance also lists perils not covered by your policy. Also known as policy exclusions, homeowners insurance generally will not pay for damage caused by flooding, earthquakes, normal wear and tear, poor maintenance and intentional acts."

Let's take Hurricane Sandy as a case study. Almost ten years ago, on October 29, 2012, Sandy took New York and several surrounding states by storm—literally. In a 48-hour period of high winds and heavy rains, hundreds of homes were destroyed. Billions of dollars of property was damaged, and some of it has yet to be fully replaced or repaired. Power outages were everywhere, including my home. And lastly, people will remember the gas lines.

SuperStorm Sandy hit my home on a Sunday night, and everyone was out of commission by Monday morning.

Believe it or not, Sandy was supposed to be much more devastating. Sandy began as a Category 3 storm, but by the time it hit New York, it was downgraded to Category 1. Why does this matter? A home insurance policy typically will have two deductibles. An all peril deductible and a hurricane deductible.

The all peril deductible is typically $1,000, while the hurricane can be anywhere from 2% to 10% of the dwelling coverage on your policy. For the purposes of this book, let's say that your hurricane deductible is 5% of your Coverage A or dwelling coverage. If your home is covered for $500,000, you are responsible for the first 5% or t$25,000, and the insurance company is responsible for everything above that.

Here is an example to bring this point to light. Let's say that strong winds from a Category 3 storm completely rips the roof off your house, and the estimate to repair the roof is $25,000. In this case, you are fully responsible to repair or replace your roof out of your own pockets. Realistically, if the wind rips off our roof, the rain that follows will cause significant interior damage to your floors, walls, furniture, etc., and the insurance company will take responsibility for paying all expenses above your hurricane deductible.

Fortunately, Hurricane Sandy had downgraded to "Tropical Storm Sandy," and the hurricane deductible did not come into play. I mentioned earlier that I lost power in my home, but I didn't lose power in my office. Our office became a triage operation to handle claims. Not only did we handle our claims; we also assisted clients insured with other agents and other companies.

At the time, my office was located on the Lower Level of BJ's Metro Mall in Middle Village, New York. Our client base is built on people in the RGMVM (Ridgewood, Glendale, Middle Village and Maspeth) area of Queens County, New York. We were ten minutes east of Brooklyn, but we also did considerable business with customers from South Queens, North Queens, and the Rockaway Peninsula. For people reading this book outside of the New York City area, think of the popular TV sitcom, *King of Queens*, starring Kevin James.

Hurricane Sandy hit my home on a Sunday night at about 7:00 p.m. We lost power but did not suffer any property damage. We returned to the office two days later on Halloween, October 31, 2012. I brought my wife and then eight-year-old son to work with me, because we had no power or heat at home. I then doubled back to pick up my staff. There was no gas available anywhere, and they would not have been able to make it to work. Writing this now and picturing people standing in gas lines still gives me nightmares. How are people supposed to prepare for this part? Should we have had auto fuel stored away at home in case of emergency?

When natural disasters hit, business as usual is thrown out the window. Our normal job as a local insurance agency is to service the clients and make every effort to write new policies. Not on that day. Not for the next two months. Our singular focus was to deliver on the promises that we sell. I informed my team that we were no longer in the insurance sales business. We did a quick study on all the key coverages. What claims would be covered? Which claims would be denied? We researched alternatives too, such as the Federal Emergency Management Assistance (FEMA) program to see how we could help when people had claims that were not covered.

Most importantly, we decided to help everyone. It did not matter if they were insured by us personally, or fellow agents from the carrier that I represent. While I lost heat and power, I have agent friends who live in the Rockaway Peninsula. They crawled to shelter in the top floors of their home, while the bottom was submerged in water. Not only did they suffer massive personal damage to their house. Their offices were also destroyed by Superstorm Sandy. It did not matter if they were insured by local agents from my respected competitors, or if they were covered by an online carrier and did not have access to a local professional office to help.

Natural disasters. High winds and raging water. Power outages. Billions of dollars of property damage. Flooding. Cars totaled because they were submerged under water. Roofs ripped off the top of the home. Siding torn off houses. Flooding. Oh my God, the flooding. Trees falling on houses. Sheds gone. Water rushing inside of houses. Every piece of furniture was destroyed by the salt water from the Atlantic Ocean. Family photos. Gone. Everybody wants property near the water. Nobody wants the water to show up in the kitchen as an uninvited guest. Food spoilage. The odor. Let's not talk about the smell. Carpets ruined. Wood floors buckled. Nicely painted walls—forget about it. What can you do? Where are you going to live when your house is uninhabitable?

Two months prior to the storm, I visited one of my clients with a beautiful home on the Rockaway Peninsula. This ranch style home in a gated community was within walking distance to the beach. We sat, had coffee, and I listened to the story of their marriage, family, careers, and the role this beautiful house played in giving them a great place to raise their kids. Senior citizens now still enjoyed the scenic views and relationships with neighbors. The conversation included intimate details on the handy work in choosing this wood over that wood, all the small improvements they made over the years to give it the perfect nautical look. We reviewed all their policies that they had bundled: home insurance, flood insurance, auto insurance, life insurance, and a Personal Umbrella Policy. All the coverages were adequate, and we did not make any notable policy changes.

As I said earlier, water does not respect people or property. Superstorm Sandy attacked every marriage memory they created in the past fifty years. Not only did the wind and water attack their home quickly; the salt water stayed around long enough to penetrate their photo albums and shred precious pictures. About a week after the storm, they were in my office. They showed me pictures taken of the damage with their iPad. I could not believe this was the same house I was in two months earlier.

Have you ever had a proud moment and a sad moment at the same time? I was deeply saddened by the damage Sandy did to all their material things, but I was also extremely proud that they were completely covered. We paid out thousands of dollars for Dwelling Damage, several thousand dollars for mold, Additional Living Expenses, unscheduled personal property and damages to other structures on their property. We also paid off two late model cars that were totaled after being submerged under water. Yes, they were in good hands.

Everyone was not as prepared and therefore not as fortunate as this couple. Countless articles have been written about what insurance companies did and did not do to handle claims related to this catastrophe. Ten years later, there are still people who have not had their homes repaired or replaced. FEMA has also been scrutinized for their response to Superstorm Sandy. At the end of the day, if there is finger pointing to be done with a scapegoat to be found, I have no problem picking out the true culprit in a police lineup.

Picture a police lineup from your favorite TV show. My two favorites are *Law and Order SVU* and *Chicago PD*. Imagine six suspects standing behind the glass with a

NATURAL DISASTERS

number from 1 to 6 hanging center mass across their chest. Here is where this exercise gets harder. All the suspects are the same race, same height, same weight, same eye-color, same sex. You do not want to blame the wrong person for not properly insuring and protecting homeowners from natural disasters. But at the same time, we cannot keep letting people take huge losses for natural events that destroy their property, and no one ever pays a price or learns a lesson, so here we go.

Let's use one letter to identify the suspects and their role in the process.

The "R" is suspect number one. The R stands for Realtor. He/She sold the property and should have told the homebuyer what kind of insurance they need.

The "L" is suspect number two. The "L" stands for Lender. She/He pays the insurance out of the mortgage every year. She/he should know what is going on and warn the homebuyer!

Suspect number 3 gets an "F." The "F" stands for FEMA. They know that something is causing more natural disasters, and everyone should carry flood insurance.

Suspect number 4 is labeled with the letter "I." The "I" is for the Insurance Company and their representatives. Surely, they know what is going on and can do more to help.

Suspect number 5 bears the scarlet letter "C." And you guessed it, "C" stands for customer. Every year the

62

company sends a renewal policy, and the customer is free to read the policy from cover to cover and make any necessary changes.

The sixth and final suspect has the letter "A." Better known as "EA" in some circles because it stands for Education and Awareness. With all that we have learned in the past ten years since Hurricane Sandy, shouldn't there be ongoing Education and Awareness campaigns to better prepare people to have the right insurance coverage in case of natural disasters?

I am pointing all ten of my fingers at suspect number 6—Education and Awareness. Suspects one through five do not get to walk away without some blame and responsibility. All five parties have a key role in increasing education and awareness. This book is both a conversation starter and a Firestarter at the same time. Let's start this conversation and see what we can do to help. I do not have all the answers, but I'm ready, willing, and able to ask tough questions.

Key Take aways

1. When it is time to perform, the time to prepare is over.
2. What are the major storms that you remember and why?
3. A covered peril is a risk or cause of loss that an insurance company will pay a claim for.
4. More education and awareness are needed to make sure people are properly insured and protected from natural disasters.

CHAPTER 7

The Annual Policy Review

> *"The number one thing you should look for is an insurance agent that offers a robust complete Annual Policy Review. This is the essence of the Kevin Spann Brand."*
>
> *- Kevin Spann*

If you put a gun to my head and said, "Kevin, what's the number one thing that we should look for when buying a property insurance policy?" Without any hesitation or reservation, I would say select an agent with an insurance company that offers a robust annual policy review. This is the essence of the Kevin Spann Brand of insuring your property dreams. We not only feel a deep personal connection to our clients when they buy a policy from our agency. We feel a HUGE personal obligation to review the policy with you once a year to make sure the policy keeps up with your ever-changing life.

Home insurance relationships often begin with first-time homebuyers who are cash strapped and need to get through the closing process with a policy that meets the DTI (debt-to-income) ratio recommended, and in some cases required by the lender. We get that and work diligently with new clients and referral partners to make sure we offer the best coverage at the best possible rate.

While fulfilling this requirement, we also do our due diligence and tell clients exactly what they are covered for and what they are not covered for today. We always tell people about two major coverages that are not a standard coverage in a home insurance policy. First, home insurance does not include flood insurance. If you are living in a high-risk flood zone or near a flood zone and are worried about the potential of your home flooding, we can and should talk about a flood insurance policy. We do not push anyone to purchase anything that is unnecessary. We simply inform them of what is included and what is excluded from this policy.

Secondly, mortgage protection life insurance is not automatically included in a home insurance policy. In other words, the policy does not include coverage that will pay off the mortgage in the event of death or the disability of the breadwinner. If two or more people buy property together, and they depend on each other's income to make the monthly payments, they should consider a mortgage protection life insurance policy to better protect their investment. It is not required as a condition of closing on the home. However, it is recommended that mortgage protection life insurance should be purchased as soon as funds are available to do so.

We plant the seeds of our annual policy review process at the inception of the policy and never let go until it blossoms into a full-grown relationship. All insurance companies mail or now email renewal policies to clients 30 to 45 days prior to the policy renewal. Usually, the buck stops there. If clients notice a premium increase or a bold print policy change that jumps off the page, they will call the company and ask questions. If no changes are noticed, most people renew their policy year after year without a second thought about what is and is not covered.

We not only tell customers that they will be contacted for an annual review, but we actually do it. How? We proactively reach out to clients with a multi-channel approach. This includes mail, e-mail, and a telephone call. All three steps are done with one end goal in mind, to schedule an appointment to review your policy. I think one is the worst number in business. If you try to decide which method of communication is best, you lose. The truth of the matter is everyone is extremely busy doing whatever they do for work, relaxation, or entertainment. If you only mail, only email, or only call, you will miss most people. However, if you do all three, you are more likely to reach people with their preferred method of communication.

What do we talk about once we schedule the appointment to review your home insurance policy? The conversation starter is always your contact information and preferred method of communication. Are all the phone numbers we have on file still correct? Do we have an email address that goes directly to your phone? Have you saved our contact information on your phone, so you can contact us in the event of a claim or other emergency? Do we have an Emergency Contact on file (someone you know and trust to contact us in the event of a claim)? Think about it. If you are injured in an accident, catastrophe, or other natural disaster, who knows what company you are insured with that you trust to file a claim on your behalf.

Let's talk more about how much contact information has changed in the past fifteen years, before we delve further into the meat of policy coverages, discounts, and riders. Has any of your contact information changed in the past fifteen years? Do you still have a landline in your house? Or was that phone number simply something you bundled to get a discount on your cable TV? Do you have your current email address on file with your home insurance company? Do they still have the "AOL" or "Hotmail" email account? Or did you give them your current g-mail account that you use now that the pandemic forced you to order food, groceries, and buy new clothing online?

Here is my biggest pet peeve: What is the name of your home insurance company or local insurance agent? This is an open book quiz. You can search your phone for help. Hopefully, you have it saved in a few places under "Insurance," "House Insurance," and the actual agent or company name. If you do not, please stop reading for a moment and find your home insurance policy. I will wait. No problem, take your time.

Here are a few hints. Although your mortgage company makes the annual payments on your home insurance company, the lender is not your insurance carrier. If you are recalling your carrier, access your mortgage loan account online and look for a tab that says, "Escrow Account." Your lender pays the annual premium on your home insurance policy through the escrow account. Find the name of that company and call or email to request a copy of your most recent declaration page. This exercise will give you the name and all the contact information for your actual insurance company. And by the way, the declaration page will also have a detailed disclosure of all your key coverages – Dwelling, Other Structures, Personal Property Protection, Guest Medical Protection, Family or Personal Liability Protection, and Loss of Use or Additional Living Expenses.

One other thing. The declaration page will also give you the annual premium for your home insurance policy.

Below is an inflation beater exercise that will help you save money.

1. Write down how much you are currently paying for your annual home insurance premium. _____

2. How many years ago did you move into your home? _____

3. How much were you paying for home insurance when you moved in ___ years ago? _____

4. How much has you home insurance increased in the past ___ years? _____

5. Did your insurance company/agent contact you at any point in the past ___ years to offer you a policy review? _____

If you have been in your house for more than ten years, don't be surprised to learn that your home insurance has increased by more than fifty percent during this same period. Some of the mortgage payment increases you endured over the years may have been related to interest rate increases, or a rise in property tax costs. Other increases may have come directly from an increase in your home insurance costs.

Here is the good news. The power of the annual review goes beyond updating contact information. The bulk of the policy review is spent discussing key coverages, new coverages, policy discounts, liability limits and riders that you may or may not want to take advantage of.

One of the tools we use during the policy review process is a Risk Assessment Calculator. We use this to make sure that your current policy limits are in line with your current assets to protect you from unforeseen accidents, catastrophes, natural disasters, and lawsuits. We ask questions to determine the market value of your current home. We also inquire about any additional properties that you may own and the value of those properties. One of my favorite questions is, "Thinking about all of your assets, what could a good lawyer sue you for?"

I know. Very uncomfortable, but very necessary. Most people do not think about getting sued, but it happens every day. My number one job is not to give you the cheapest policy I can find. My primary job is to properly protect your dreams with the right products to properly cover your assets.

Did I mention yet that your property insurance policy comes fully equipped with a lawyer? My bad. If you are ever sued personally, report it to your insurance company. They will hire a lawyer to defend you. If you lose the lawsuit, the insurance company will pay out up to the liability limits on your policy. This should make you feel better, but you cannot relax. At least not yet.

Liability is an insurance industry word that simply means "responsibility." The minimum liability limit on most property insurance policies is $100,000. I know what you are thinking, "Sounds good to me, Kevin. Stop writing and don't scare me anymore." Unfortunately, I cannot. Median home values increased from $79,000 in 1990 to $119,000 in 2000. They almost doubled to $220,000 in 2010 and peaked at $423,000 nationwide in the fourth quarter of 2021.

What does this have to do with your home insurance? A good lawyer can sue you based on your net worth. It does not matter if you do not have two nickels to rub together. If your net worth is a million dollars, you need to be insured like a millionaire.

I insure a lot of people that I like to think of as "accidental millionaires." These are working people with middle-class jobs and a middle-class lifestyle, who simply bought the right house in the right neighborhood at the right time. Their net worth has grown on pace with the housing market boom. If they contributed to the company retirement plan consistently and rode the wave off the stock market, their assets may have grown north of seven figures in this area as well.

I mentioned that minimum liability limits on a home insurance policy start at $100,000. Family Liability limits generally max out at $1,000,000 on a traditional home insurance policy. We suggest Personal Umbrella Policies (PUP) to all our accidental millionaires. For a few hundred dollars a year, a policyholder can buy a PUP policy that provides excess liability coverage above and beyond what is offered on their home insurance policy and their auto insurance policy as well.

The time to buy a PUP is before you need it. You cannot buy car insurance after the accident. You cannot buy house insurance while the house is on fire. And you cannot buy life insurance on your deathbed. Here is a story to better make this point.

The first chance I had to sell a PUP policy was in 2007, shortly after starting my agency. A gentleman walked in and asked for a PUP policy before anything else. As a new business owner with heavy overhead, my heart leaped at the sales opportunity. In order to buy a PUP policy, a client has to carry certain minimum liability limits on their Home Insurance and Auto Insurance policy. I thought, *Yes! I'm starting to get excited! This is going to be a three or four item deal, can't wait!* I started my fact finding, which was simply gathering basic information about all drivers on the car policy, basic details about the home, and most importantly, why.

Leaning in, I asked what was in the market for a PUP? He leaned across my desk and whispered gently, "I killed someone in a car accident last year. I'm being sued. My wife and family don't know anything about it, and you can't say anything." I offered my empathy, made limited eye contact, and continued to complete the application. Next question: "Are you currently being sued? (If yes, not eligible for a policy at this time).

When it is time to perform, the time to prepare is over. Fifteen years later, I have never forgotten the look in his eyes. Obviously, he was devastated being involved in a fatality and felt terrible about what happened. Now he would have to deal with the financial devastation as well—but all alone.

I am often motivated by the ones that got away. Athletes state the losses stay with them longer than the wins. I never judged or blamed him for what happened in the car accident. It can happen to any of us in the blink of an eye. Take your eyes off the road for one second and a kid or an adult with earbuds in and their eyes glued to whatever they are doing, can walk right in front of your car and BOOM! When a vehicle makes contact with a passenger, a bike, or a pet, there is no debate about who is at fault. The onus is always on the driver to prevent the accident.

Annual policy reviews are challenging but very necessary. The essence of the review is to talk about what has changed in a client's life in the past year(s) since we last reviewed the policy. Change is the only constant for every client. We have changes in our family, occupation, recreational activities, and our dreams. The beauty of having a long-term business relationship is working with someone that you can get to know and trust over time.

Sometimes, discounts can be the highlight of the annual policy review. Bundling is always the biggest and best way to save money. People are always excited when you bundle their car insurance with their home insurance and discover the savings can be upwards of 35% on their policy. It is something about having more coverage for less money that really resonates with people. We also inquire about alarm discounts. Has there been any change in your occupation? Often, retirees and senior citizens can receive ample cost-savings on a policy. Renovations and upgrades to the major systems in your house, such as the plumbing, electrical system, HVAC, and roof can also greatly reduce a policy.

Riders are the final part of the annual policy review discussion. We always recommend the maximum amount of water backup coverage to protect our clients against the risks of having their basements and lower-level floors from being destroyed by sewage water backing up into their basement and running rampant on lower-level floors.

Not all the conversations are technical. We love asking friendly questions like: Did you treat yourself to any new jewelry since your last birthday or the most recent holiday season? This inquiry opens conversations about the policy limits for certain items. For example, most jewelry coverage is limited to $1,000 or in some cases $2,500 per item. We then present options of insuring their jewelry on their home insurance policy or insuring with a specialized carrier like Jeweler's Mutual Insurance Company. It is always about protecting other people's dreams. It is never about simply upselling or simply increasing our bottom line.

"Everything must change. Nothing stays the same. Everyone will change. No one stays the same." The opening line of this Nina Simone song is appropriate to include here. Just as the lyrics to the song suggests, things are always changing and that is the driving force behind the annual policy review. The Annual Policy Review is the core of the Kevin Spann Brand of insuring your property insurance. The price of the policies we offer become a factor when we do not offer sufficient value. We are always striving to increase the value of what we offer to clients, prospects, former clients, and referral partners.

Key Take aways

1. The Annual Policy Review is the essence of the Kevin Spann Brand.
2. Flood Insurance and Mortgage Protection Life Insurance are never included in a standard home insurance policy.
3. An annual policy review should introduce new coverages and discuss all current available discounts.
4. A Personal Umbrella Policy (PUP) is an excess liability policy to protect clients from unforeseen accidents, lawsuits, catastrophes, and natural disasters.

EPILOGUE

Plan. Prepare. Perform.

Homeownership is a dream for some and a reality for others. The Abraham Kevin Spann & Sons Insurance Agency plans to insure as many of these dreams as we possibly can. When we quote or review policies from our respected competitors, we are open, honest, and encourage people to stay where they are, but you might want to tweak or adjust this, that, or something else. People seem to respect and appreciate this approach.

When it comes to insurance, people have unlimited choices. Finding cheap insurance is as easy as finding cheap fast food. There is always a cheaper burger, but sometimes you want a grass-fed Kobe burger, personally prepared for you with all the trimmings and a glass of your favorite wine. The price only matters if the value of the Kobe burger does not exceed your drive-thru experience at your favorite fast-food joint.

We touched every topic from key property insurance coverages to a colorful conversation about claims. Hopefully, this conversation struck a nerve and will help you, your

Epilogue

family, and friends take action and demand more service, education, and awareness from your current insurance carrier.

You now know enough to be dangerous. Test your new powers on your current carrier. Ask them, "What am I not covered for on this policy?" If they cannot answer this question, run. I will be waiting to hear from you.

Made in the USA
Columbia, SC
13 August 2023

21546874R00057